D1510457

FABERGÉ
EGGS

FABERGÉ
EGGS

Grange BOOKS

A QUANTUM BOOK

Published by Grange Books
an imprint of Grange Books Plc
The Grange
Kingsnorth Industrial Estate
Hoo, nr. Rochester
Kent ME3 9ND

Copyright ©1999 Quantum Books Ltd

All rights reserved.
This book is protected by copyright. No part of it may be
reproduced, stored in a retrieval system, or transmitted in
any form or by any means, without the prior permission in
writing of the Publisher, nor be otherwise circulated in any
form of binding or cover other than that in which it is
published and without a similar condition including this
condition being imposed on the subsequent publisher.

1-84013-284-1

This book is produced by
Quantum Books Ltd
6 Blundell Street
London N7 9BH

Project Manager: Rebecca Kingsley
Project Editor: Judith Millidge
Designer: Wayne Humphries
Editor: Clare Haworth-Maden

The material in this publication previously appeared in
The Art of Faberge

QUMFBEG
Set in Times
Reproduced in Singapore by Eray Scan (Pte) Ltd
Printed in Singapore by Star Standard Industries (Pte) Ltd

CONTENTS

INTRODUCTION

The extraordinary success of Peter Carl Fabergé in his lifetime, and the fact that he is remembered when other excellent craftsmen have been forgotten, can be explained in a number of ways: his work reflects the highest traditions of European applied art; he used only the finest materials and employed the best craftsmen to carry out his ideas; and, finally, there is a crucial element that distinguishes his work from that of others – a unique quality that has come to be expressed in one word – Fabergé.

Opposite: Superbly crafted pieces by Fabergé, typical of those displayed in the homes of the upper classes in Russia and Britain around the turn of the century. The yellow-enamelled-guilloche case of the clock is inscribed inside the door '2 Mai 1898, Alexis'. The Grand Duke Alexis Alexandrovitch was the fourth son of Alexander III.

THE HISTORY OF THE HOUSE OF FABERGÉ
Fabergé. The name conjures up images of unbelievable splendour and unimaginable opulence. Against the backdrop of the sumptuous, glittering world of the last tsars of Russia, here was a man who dedicated his life to the creation of priceless treasures for the Imperial family, a task in which cost and time had no significance, in which gaining Imperial approval was all.

So runs the legend, and there is much truth in it, but this is by no means the whole story.

Below: The plush interior of the House of Fabergé's St Petersburg showroom, presided over by Fabergé himself, who had a small office at the rear, from which vantage point he was able to observe his clients coming and going.

Below: The cases which contained the precious objects from Fabergé were created with as much care as the objects themselves. They were made of polished holly by craftsmen and lined with padded white silk stamped with the Imperial warrant.

Fabergé lived through one of the most momentous periods in the history of Russia, but his work reflected earlier traditions of devoted service and noble patronage that were rooted in the eighteenth century. The calm, patient values of the master craftsman so evident in his work were maintained at a time when Russia was on the point of cataclysmic eruption; a period of change that had lasted for more than a century and was about to erupt in the Russian Revolution of 1917.

Peter Carl Fabergé, who has been described as the last of the great goldsmiths, was born in St Petersburg on 30 May 1846. His father, Gustav Fabergé, was a jeweller with a small but prosperous shop in Bolshaya Morskaya Street, St Petersburg. The family's French name can be traced back to seventeenth-century France and the reign of Louis XIV. Of Huguenot stock, they were persecuted and, like others of the faith, had to flee the country. They moved east and finally settled in Russia. Having changed their name to Fabri or Favri during their travels, they felt secure enough to revert to the original name of Fabergé in the eighteenth century, when Carl's grandfather, Peter, became a Russian subject in the Baltic province of Estonia. It was there, in the town of Pernau, that Carl's father, Gustav, was born in 1814.

The Fabergé family was evidently in a reasonable way of business because Peter Carl (Carl Gustavovitch in Russian) was able to attend one of the best schools in St Petersburg. Fabergé's education was planned with his future career in mind. After schooling, he took a commercial course at the *Handelschule* in Dresden, Germany, where he was confirmed at the age of 15 in 1861.

FABERGÉ'S EARLY DAYS

Fabergé's early training as a goldsmith also began in Germany, where he was apprenticed to a leading German goldsmith, Friedmann, at Frankfurt-am-Main. It was at this time that he made his European Grand Tour, an event which Fabergé scholars believe had a great influence on his future artistic development. With a friend, Jules Butz, the son of a successful St Petersburg jeweller, he visited Italy and France. In Florence, with its abundance of treasures, he is known to have visited the famous centre of hardstone-carving, the Opificio delle Pietre Dure, and would certainly

have seen the Medici collection of enamelled jewels and hardstone vessels. In Paris, he witnessed for himself the results of the great flowering of French eighteenth-century jewellery, which was to have a profound effect on his future work. So by the time that Fabergé took over the modest family business in Morskaya Street in 1870, at the age of 24, he was well equipped, having had both commercial and artistic training.

A DARING SWITCH OF STYLE

When Fabergé took over the firm, it was a small, well-established business which someone else might have been happy merely to manage. Instead, he decided on a daring switch of style, from the heavy, obviously expensive jewellery then popular, to something lighter, in which the design of the object was more important than the intrinsic value of the materials used. The move was surprising, even revolutionary, given the spirit of the time.

There was a shift, too, from the use of precious stones and metals to less expensive stones and natural minerals from Russia: the deep-green jade of nephrite, the glistening black of obsidian, the purity of rock crystal, the warm, tawny shades of aventurine quartz. Even wood from the forests of Russia was used by this daring jeweller: Karelian birch, palisander, white holly. The latter was highly polished and used for Fabergé boxes, which became almost trademarks, works of craftsmanship and beauty to enclose precious objects. The point about these materials was that they were selected only for their suitability in the design, not because they were of value.

Traditional jewellery was still made, but the *objets de fantasie* (traditional *objets d'art* combined with functional items, meticulously made and stamped with a particular style) encapsulated the impulse of creativity for which the House of Fabergé came to be known. This Fabergé style is easy to recognise but difficult to define. It has a kind of assured, restrained elegance and is notable for the quality of the unobtrusive craftsmanship, seen in hinges which are virtually invisible and work effortlessly, in the depths of colour of *guilloche* enamel, in the subtle ways in which different colours of gold are worked and combined. It reflects a period when time

Below: A superb example of the skill of Fabergé's first head workmaster, Erik Kollin, this Scythian gold bracelet made in 1882 is a copy of one of the treasures from 400 BC which were discovered in the Crimea in 1867. It is made of yellow gold with lion finials and won the firm its first international gold medal when it was exhibited at the Pan-Russian Exhibition in 1882.

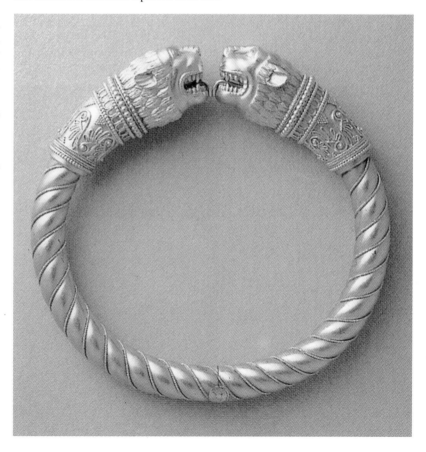

was unimportant in the achievement of the desired effect, when patience was a necessary part of creating a beautiful object and when hours were not calculated or allowed to affect the decision to make something or not.

THE HOUSE OF FABERGÉ PROSPERS

The new style of work was evidently popular and the House of Fabergé prospered, but although he initiated a new approach in the craft of the jeweller and goldsmith, Fabergé looked for inspiration, particularly in his early years, to the antique world. His reputation became more widely known when he was invited to make copies of a number of Scythian treasures, ornaments from 400 BC which had been found at Kersh in the Crimea in 1867 by Count Sergei Stroganov. The results were so remarkable that the tsar was unable to see any difference between Fabergé's work and the originals. The work was carried out by Fabergé's first workmaster, Erik Kollin, a Finn who worked exclusively for Fabergé from 1870 and whose work often contains elements taken from antiquity.

The copies of the Scythian treasures were a great success when they were exhibited at the Nuremberg Fair of 1885, and Fabergé was awarded the gold medal, a success that followed his gold medal at the Pan-Russian Exhibition in 1882. Further honours followed, and his international reputation was established beyond dispute. There is no doubt, however, that the most crucial event in Fabergé's career was his appointment as court jeweller in 1885. Imperial patronage was conferred by Alexander III, and with the appointment began one of the most astonishing examples of the goldsmith's art, the Imperial Easter eggs, a commission which was to last for more than 30 years. The exact circumstances of the commissioning of the first Imperial egg are not known, but there is a rather touching story that the intimidating Alexander III wished to give his wife, Marie, a Danish princess, a present that would remind her of home, and so Fabergé created an egg that was a copy of one in the Danish Royal Collection.

Inset: Fabergé's first Imperial Easter egg, made in 1885 (6.3cm/2½in). The shell is of opaque white enamel with a gold interior and it holds a gold chicken with ruby eyes. The hen originally contained a surprise of a crown set with diamonds and a ruby but this has been lost.

Right: The gold Easter egg in the Danish Royal Collection, Copenhagen, made in the first half of the eighteenth century, is believed to have inspired Fabergé's first Imperial Easter egg. Some experts, however, believe that there may not be a direct connection, as similar eggs were made in other parts of Europe – two can be found in Vienna and Dresden. The Danish egg has a white ivory shell and contains an enamelled gold chicken with diamond eyes, which opens to reveal a crown set with pearls and diamonds and a diamond-set ring.

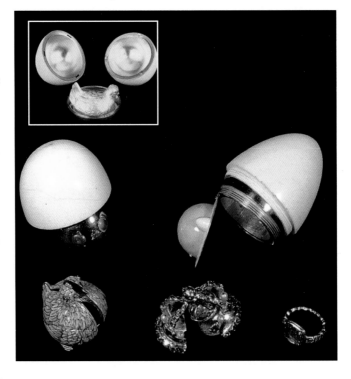

THE IMPERIAL SEAL OF APPROVAL

The gift was obviously a success, for it was decreed that a similar creation should be presented every year. This single act of patronage, made without reference to price, gave the House of Fabergé the security to attempt the extraordinary levels of invention and craftsmanship which were necessary. Because the essential element of the Imperial egg was its surprise, hidden inside the egg itself, some took years to make.

The patronage continued after Alexander III died peacefully in 1894 and was succeeded by Nicholas II, his son. Nicholas extended the commission, ruling that there should be two Imperial eggs each year: one for the Dowager Empress Marie Feodorovna, and one for his wife, the Tsarina Alexandra Feodorovna.

The title of court jeweller was not a courtesy title and the Imperial eggs were but the pinnacle of a string of commissions to meet the needs and obligations of the court. There were innumerable objects required to mark anniversaries of institutions and families; or for tributes to individuals and groups; gifts to visiting or departing statesmen and to regiments; or in recognition of acts of service by all manner of people, rewards to the great and small – a stream of gifts that would engage much of the skills and energies of the House of Fabergé as jewellers, goldsmiths and silversmiths. There were the personal gifts needed by the Imperial family, their birthdays, christenings and weddings to be remembered. Then there was a vast and intricate web of family relationships linking the Romanov family to the royal families of Europe, especially those of Great Britain, Denmark and Germany, all of whom would appreciate some item stamped with the maker's mark: Fabergé.

PATRONAGE BY THE RICH AND ELITE

With Imperial approval came the approval of the merely rich, who felt it essential that they, too, should be able to point proudly to their own collection of Fabergé. Among these was the fabulously wealthy Alexander Kelch, a Siberian gold millionaire who was an enthusiastic patron of Fabergé, ordering several fine pieces and a number of eggs, similar to those made for the Imperial family, for his wife, Barbara; these are known as the 'Kelch Eggs'. Madame Kelch had a fondness for large and precious stones, a fondness indulged by her husband, and Fabergé supplied many sumptuous examples, including a superb necklace in which the stone weighed 30 carats.

The old, aristocratic families naturally patronised the court jeweller: Fabergé made an Easter egg in the Imperial style that was

Below: The 'Coronation Egg', presented by Tsar Nicholas II to his wife, the Tsarina Alexandra Feodorovna in 1897, is one of the most stunning of all the Imperial eggs. It is a perfect example of the exquisite craftsmanship and imagination of the House of Fabergé. All the Imperial eggs contained a 'surprise', and in this egg it is a miniature of the coronation coach, a perfect copy of the original, which took a painstaking 15 months to make.

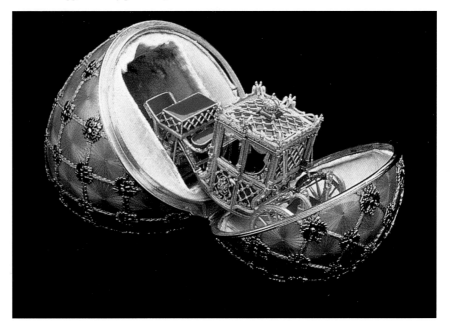

Below: A smoky-quartz goblet standing on a reeded-gold base. Made by head workmaster Michael Perchin, it was a gift from a Russian grand duke to the famous ballerina Madame Elizabeth Balletta, of the Imperial Michael Theatre, St Petersburg. Elegant and serene, it was described by Fabergé's first biographer, Henry Bainbridge, as 'perhaps the most beautiful thing Fabergé ever made'.

given by Prince Felix Youssoupov to his wife, Zenaide, to celebrate their twenth-fifth wedding anniversary.

Another favoured customer for whom Fabergé made an egg in the Imperial style was Dr Emanuel Nobel, a wealthy Swedish businessman living in Russia (he was the nephew of Alfred Nobel, the inventor of dynamite, who is now remembered for the Nobel prize). Nobel was a generous host and he was rich enough to give full rein to his instincts. He enjoyed bestowing trinkets from Fabergé on the ladies at his dinner table; on one occasion they were presented with pendants and brooches made of rock crystal and frosted with diamonds,

which resembled magnified snowflakes.

There were gifts for the stars of the artistic world of St Petersburg, the heroines of the ballet and theatre who were idolised by rich and importunate admirers and showered with precious gifts. Benois remembered how the ballerina Zucchi received the wild adulation of the audience after one performance, almost completely disappearing under innumerable bouquets of flowers, and how, at the climax of the celebration, she was presented with an open box containing a necklace of enormous diamonds, a gift from her admirer, Prince Vassiltchikov, which was rumoured to be worth 30,000 roubles. Elizabeth Balletta, prima ballerina at the Imperial Michael Theatre, St Petersburg, was given a superb rock-crystal goblet by a Russian grand duke, a gift described by Henry Bainbridge, Fabergé's first biographer, as 'perhaps the most beautiful thing Fabergé had ever made'. Kchessinskaya, also of the St Petersburg ballet, had a Fabergé collection, while Fabergé made a diamond setting for a brooch of Karsavina's, a superb Siberian amethyst, one of a set which had originally been presented by Catherine the Great to Count Zubov.

FABERGÉ'S FAME SPREADS

The fame of the House of Fabergé spread to Great Britain as the result of gifts sent by the Romanovs to their English family, in particular by Marie Feodorovna, dowager empress of Russia, to her sister, Queen Alexandra. The pleasure-loving Edward VII admired the work of Fabergé enough to ensure that many of his wife's birthday presents came from him, and he also presented Fabergé souvenirs to other ladies who gained royal approval – very many of them, by all accounts.

Edward's enthusiasm was taken up by the

fashionable world of Edwardian England, and the cream of society demonstrated their sense of chic by buying from the House of Fabergé. Indeed, the enthusiasm for Fabergé was such that a London branch was opened in the early years of the twentieth century. Crowned heads of Europe, earls, dukes, great ladies of fashion – all wanted to possess some unique object from the master goldsmith.

Chulalongkorn, the King of Siam, was an admirer and had several important pieces made, while many of the unbelievably wealthy maharajahs of India and the mandarins of China were also enthusiastic customers.

THE BUSINESS EXPANDS

The House of Fabergé was so successful that it became necessary to expand to cope with the flood of business. By 1890 the premises in Morskaya Street had doubled in size and a Moscow branch was opened in 1897, with branches at Odessa and Kiev opening in the following years. Greater changes came in 1898 when a new building was bought at 24 Morskaya Street, which was designed to house the many functions of the Fabergé empire.

At this period about 500 people were employed, producing thousands of articles to meet an apparently insatiable demand. What is extraordinary is that, despite so many hands, the pieces have a distinctive character, an individual style, a personality that was a result of the watchful presence of Fabergé himself, the benign ruler of this expanding empire. This uniformity of style is all the more astonishing when the range of objects created by Fabergé is considered. At the head of the output may be placed the Imperial Easter eggs, but they are, in truth, only a tiny fraction of the work of the House of Fabergé, as are the highly prized flowers and figurines and hardstone-

carvings, if they are considered against the vast outpouring of objects which adorned the residences of the fashionable at home and abroad – clocks, barometers, cigarette-holders, match-holders, picture frames, scent bottles, bell pushes, lorgnettes, opera glasses, letter-openers, hat pins, buckles, boxes of all kinds, crochet hooks, desk sets, ink-holders, paper knives, stamp-dispensers, glue pots, *bonbon-nières*, cigarette cases and more. The cigarette cases, for example, were made with such craftsmanship and style that they are as sought after today as they were when they were made; as Fabergé's equivalent of the magnificent snuffboxes of the eighteenth century, they elevated a functional object to a higher plane and delighted the visual and tactile senses.

A WORLD IN THE PROCESS OF CHANGE

All these items shared a common identity, however simple the materials, however humdrum the use: each had the same concentration of style, the craftsmanship, the restraint and elegance that marks the work of Fabergé.

Together with all this there was the day-to-day work of any jeweller commissioned by the court: finding the most suitable stones and placing them in the finest of settings and making silverware for the Imperial table. The *Inventaire de l'Argenterie*, devoted to the silver in the possession of Nicholas II, which was published by Baron Foelkersma in 1907, describes the House of Fabergé as 'the best and most celebrated in the world'.

It was, however, a world in the process of change. The effects of Russia's disastrous war against Japan and its involvement in the First World War depleted the country's wealth and manpower. Against this backdrop of political change and economic difficulty the revolutionary ideas of the Bolsheviks took hold, and

Below: The sea-monster motif of this finely crafted rhodonite and silver candlestick appears frequently in Fabergé designs.

Below: Fabergé was a great favourite with the royal families of Russia and Britain. Pictured here is Tsar Nicholas II (standing in front of the pavilion on the left) at the Regimental March Past of the Jägereski Guards at Peterhof, 1907.

the society in which Fabergé had flourished vanished forever when the Imperial family was deposed by the revolution of 1917.

Like many Russians, Fabergé fled from his homeland and, with the help of the British Embassy, went to Germany and finally to France, where he died on 24 September 1920.

The death of the master craftsman came at the end of an era, severing the link between the opulence of Imperial Russia and the egalitarianism of the modern world. Without his presence, it was impossible for the House of Fabergé to continue creating the objects for which it had been so famous. Two of his gifted sons, Eugène and Alexander, did set up a business in Paris in 1924 under the name of Fabergé & Cie, but although several fine pieces were made the business never achieved the reputation of the original. It ceased trading in 1940. The name changed hands several times, and Fabergé still exists in Paris, specialising in

modern jewellery. A separate firm in the United States, with no connection with the original, uses the Fabergé name for a range of toiletries.

FABERGÉ TREASURES REACH THE WEST

Trading in the works of Fabergé continued to be brisk, principally from economic necessity on the part of Russians who had fled from the new regime and were selling their treasures in order to live. An important centre for trade of this kind, *La Vieille Russie*, was opened in Paris in 1920, where masterpieces by Fabergé and others were bought and sold.

Fabergé's work was well known in the West, of course, before the revolution. The English royal family had amassed a splendid collection, and examples of his art could be seen in the homes of the rich and fashionable throughout the country. But the Imperial eggs, the summit of his creativity, were not generally known because they were private gifts from Alexander III and Nicholas II to members of their family. They were not for public display and were, indeed, shown publicly only on one occasion, by special permission, at the Exposition Internationale Universelle in 1900. With the flood of rich émigrés and their treasures, and the ensuing auctions and exhibitions, the world at large gradually became aware of these extraordinary creations, which captured the public imagination as symbols of the departed glory of the Imperial Russian court.

Economic chaos in Russia after the revolution led the authorities to sell off many of the Imperial treasures to raise capital to bolster the country's finances, a decision that went against the express wish of Lenin, who said that the new authorities should preserve the nation's cultural heritage. The architect of the revolution died in 1924, however.

FABERGÉ'S WORK REACHES A WIDER PUBLIC
Stories of the fabulous wealth of the tsars circulated in the West and there were romantic tales associated with it: for example, there was the discovery of the hoard of jewels hidden in the home of Prince Youssoupov, for whom Fabergé had made one of the few Easter-egg masterpieces not intended for the Imperial family – evidence of a highly valued customer. Secret passages in the prince's palace led to a glittering hoard, itemised by Suzy Menkes in her book *Royal Jewels* as 255 brooches, 13 tiaras, 42 bracelets and 210 kilos in weight of jewelled ornaments.

A dashing young English aristocrat, Bertie Stopford, came to the aid of the Grand Duchess Vladimir in exile and rescued her magnificent collection of jewellery. Behaving with the gallantry of a fictional hero, he made his way to Russia, disguised himself as a workman, managed to infiltrate the grand duchess's former palace and retrieved the jewels. Stopford succeeded in smuggling them out of the country, via the British Embassy, wrapped in newspapers and transported in a pair of Gladstone bags.

There are many similar stories of collectors retrieving Fabergé treasures from Russia, of Dr Armand Hammer, for example, who acquired a wealth of Russian valuables, many by Fabergé, and was probably the person most responsible for making the Russian master craftsman's work known to the American public. Dr Hammer spent the years 1921 to 1930 in post-revolution Russia and became a friend of Lenin. In exchange for Hammer's efforts to set up a barter agreement with the USA, which would bring in a million tons of wheat, Lenin granted him trading concessions. During the time that Hammer and his brother, Victor, were in Russia, they acquired an outstanding collection of art treasures, including 15 of the fabulous Imperial Easter eggs, which they took back with them to the USA at the beginning of the Stalin era. Back in New York, Hammer set up the Hammer Galleries and took a travelling exhibition of 2,000 splendid items around the country. Hammer's assistant at one time was the distinguished Fabergé expert Alexander Schaffer, who made a number of visits to Russia and acquired many Fabergé items, including more Imperial eggs. He later opened a branch of *La Vieille Russie* in New York, and this remains the leading centre in the USA for the works of Fabergé. Meanwhile, Emanuel Snowman, of the London jewellers Wartski, organised an exhibition in 1927 of the treasures that he had acquired from Russian sources, and in 1935 Lady Zia Wernher, granddaughter of Nicholas II, was the guiding spirit behind a

Below left: A bonsai study of a spray of japonica emerging from a hana-ire *bamboo flowerpot, itself supported on a low Confucian scholar's table. The leaves are carved from Siberian jade, the pot from bowenite and the table from white serpentine.*

wide-ranging and influential exhibition of Russian art in London, which included over 100 works by Fabergé. Throughout this century, the art of Fabergé has been continually exhibited, ensuring that the works of the Russian master craftsman have become known to a much wider public than would have been envisaged in the days of the Imperial court or the privileged world of Edwardian society.

THE FASCINATION OF FABERGÉ

It is easy to understand the interest of art historians, designers, craftsmen and collectors in the work of Fabergé, but the fascination of the general public is harder to explain. It is possible that this fascination is prompted by the romantic associations that the works have with the last days of the tsar and the disappearance of the doomed Romanov dynasty, but it may also be that the enduing qualities of Fabergé's works, the quality of materials, the faultless workmanship, the elusive but definite sense of style, have a powerful appeal in an age in which the throwaway, the ephemeral and the plastic are paramount.

Below left: A silver-mounted nephrite dampener – part of an unusual game set. It is thought that it was used to moisten the tips of the fingers before dealing cards.

Below right: A menu-holder in aventurine and silver.

INFLUENCES, TECHNIQUES AND MATERIALS

Previous page: A Rococo clock made by Julius Rappoport for Fabergé, a copy of an English clock made by James Hagger in London in 1735.

Right: A gold and enamel cigarette case in translucent pink.

Below: A jewelled gold and enamel pendant. The central moonstone is flanked with trefoil rose-cut diamonds.

Bottom: A gold, diamond and ruby heart-shaped lady's locket.

Fabergé's description of himself as an artist-jeweller is a telling indication of his approach to his work. His best pieces show a unique alliance of the skills of the craftsman with the imagination of the artist, and it is evident that his decisions in matters of design were based on artistic judgments rather than commercial considerations. Fabergé and his craftsmen drew on an extremely wide range of influences from across the world and through the ages, which inspired their choices of design, methods and materials, and this versatility was reflected in the vast range of diverse objects which all bore the distinctive Fabergé style.

ARTIST OR CRAFTSMAN?

There has been much long and often laborious discussion among art historians about whether Fabergé can properly be called an artist or whether he is not more accurately defined as a craftsman. If the definition of an artist is a person who makes a highly individual statement, a personal act of creation, using his or her own talents in whatever the chosen medium, then Fabergé was not an artist. Instead, he was the presiding genius of a large organisation which, at its height, employed hundreds of people and produced thousands of objects which had the right to be called 'Fabergé' but were not made by his hand. Indeed, there is no evidence of any piece which was made by him or any design which was indisputably by him. But all the evidence we have – from primary sources, colleagues and members of the Fabergé family – shows the influence he wielded and how he made it possible for his booming organisation to produce a vast range of objects, all of which bore his essential, unmistakable style.

According to Bainbridge and others, Fabergé was a reticent man, but he was unusually frank during an interview with a Russian magazine *Stoliza y Usadba ('Town and Country')* in January 1914, leaving no doubt as to his view of his place in the debate about whether he was an artist or craftsman.

Clearly, if you compare my things with those of such firms as Tiffany, Boucheron and Cartier, of course you will find that the value of theirs is greater than of mine. As far as they are concerned, it is possible to find a necklace in stock for one-and-a-half million roubles. But of course these people are merchants and not artist-jewellers. Expensive things interest me little if the value is merely in so many diamonds and pearls.

History appears to have accepted his valuation of his own work, since it has not only survived but grown in popularity, while the work of his contemporaries is known only to specialists. Among the best of his competitors were craftsmen such as Ovchinnikov, a celebrated goldsmith, much of whose work exhibits wonderful examples of cloisonné enamelling in the traditional Russian style; Karl Hahn, who was also commissioned by the Imperial court and made several fine pieces, including a superb tiara in the shape of a Russian kokoshnik, the traditional peasant headdress, but made of pearls and diamonds, which was worn by Tsarina Alexandra Feodorovna at her coronation in 1896; Tillander, who made small objects for display in the style of Fabergé, and Bolin of St Petersburg, both important rivals who also carried out commissions for the Imperial court; and the 'English Shop' of De Nichols and Pinke, who were leading silversmiths.

FABERGÉ'S INFLUENCES

Fabergé's output shows a wide variety of influences, which is not surprising in such a long

Below left: A Fabergé gold and diamond brooch with a three-loop bow and tear-shaped pendants.

Below right: A two-colour-gold and enamel pendant with a chalcedony cabochon.

Below: This jewelled diadem is a fine example of Art Nouveau in Fabergé's work. The ten cyclamens in the piece are set with circular- and rose-cut diamonds and are linked by a diamond-set band. The work-master was Albert Holmström.

career as a designer, but it is always unlike that of his contemporaries, most notably in two areas: it is generally less traditional and it shows a greater sense of what may be called restraint or understatement.

When Fabergé took control of the family business in 1870, the style of work produced by goldsmiths and jewellers in Russia tended towards the heavy, ornate and ostentatious – as, indeed, it did in most of the applied arts in Europe. The precious objects made, both for wear and for display in the home, were designed to reflect the wealth of the owner through the value of the materials used. Fabergé and his brother, Agathon, decided to move away from statements of that kind,

aiming for objects whose principal value was their design, with any precious stones and materials utilised purely to suit the designer's concept and not for their intrinsic worth.

The Fabergé style was eclectic in general, but exhibits the influence of the past, using designs from various historical periods. As we know, Fabergé's artistic education was broadly based, and he had been given the opportunity to travel and study widely in Europe. Renaissance and Baroque, as well as eighteenth-century, influences are plain to see in his *oeuvre,* drawn in part from his observation of the Medici treasures in Florence and eighteenth-century art in France. Perhaps more influential was his period in Dresden and his

familiarity with the Green Vaults Collection, which contained a wide range of works, including gem-carvings from Saxon times, Renaissance enamels, as well as examples of eighteenth-century art. This collection would also, no doubt, have played a significant part in forming the ideas of his brother, Agathon, who was born in Dresden and studied there.

A closer and more accessible source of artistic inspiration for Fabergé was the Imperial Collection at the Hermitage and the Winter Palace. Here the tsars had amassed treasures from France, Italy, Germany and Russia, all of which were available to Fabergé.

ORIGINS OF THE FABERGÉ STYLE

Particularly from the early days of Fabergé's career, there are striking examples of the sources of his inspiration in the series of Imperial eggs: the first, the golden 'Hen Egg', dating from 1885, is a copy of a similar, eighteenth-century creation in the Danish Royal Collection at Rosenborg Castle, Copenhagen, while the 'Renaissance Egg' of 1894 is copied from an eighteenth-century design by Le Roy, which was in the Green Vaults Collection. Yet these are not slavish copies: although their inspiration is clear, they have a style that is pure Fabergé in its elegance and outstanding craftsmanship.

The greatest historical influence on Fabergé came from France, particularly eighteenth-century France, and he reproduced techniques used only at that time, notably the *guilloche* method of enamelling, which involves placing translucent layers of enamel on a machine-engraved surface. The method is costly and time-consuming but gives the most beautiful effects, especially in the depth of colour.

Looking at the variety of Fabergé's output, it is clear that he had a sharp eye for possible inspiration from any source. Repetition was

Below: An oval, jewelled, guilloche-*enamel and vari-coloured-gold snuffbox.*

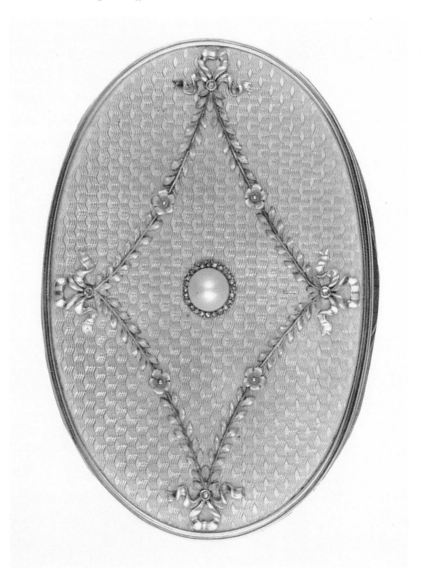

Below: Ornate designs for tableware from Fabergé. They are of special interest to scholars because they throw new light on the work of the designers, most of whom were anonymous.

to be avoided at all costs, which meant a flow of new ideas and a consequent search for more. His historical sources ranged from Gothic to Renaissance and, in his later work, Louis XVI and Empire styles. Old-Russian style was a strong influence, especially in his silverwork. Around the turn of the century he was also influenced by the school of Art Nouveau, a movement which was a reaction against the

reworking of ideas from the past and which used the world of nature as its inspiration. However, the movement had only a peripheral effect on Fabergé, although some of the silver pieces that he made in Moscow show abstract influences.

INTERPRETING THE NATURAL WORLD
His principal response to the natural world was

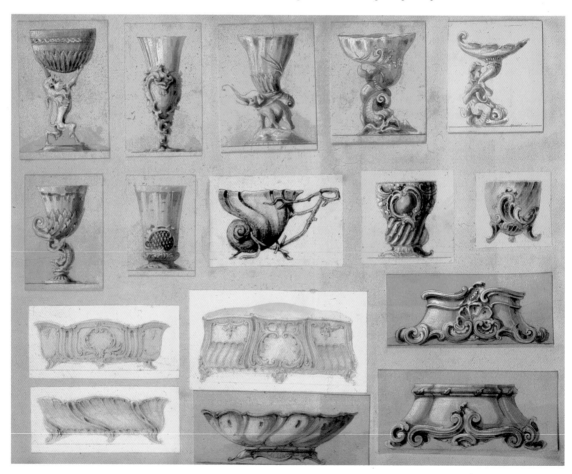

in a naturalistic form, in the creation of the superb series of flowers in precious stones and materials. These are marvellous likenesses of simple country flowers, such as lilies of the valley and bluebells. At first glance they seem to be faithful botanical reproductions, yet in fact they are not mere copies but artistic creations representing the spirit of the natural object, with a cunning use of diamonds for drops of dew and delicate gold for fragile stems.

There are echoes of the Far East in Fabergé's flower studies, and it is true that Japanese art played an important part in the Art Nouveau movement. The influence of Japanese art can also be seen in some of the small animal-carvings made in the Fabergé workshops, which are in the Japanese *netsuke* style. Fabergé had a large personal collection of over 500 pieces of Japanese *netsuke* – carved belt toggles, often made in ivory – which were originally functional but which had by then become display objects.

Fabergé was never content to work in the Russian tradition of many of the goldsmiths of his time. He was too cosmopolitan, had a wider educational background and served a more discriminating range of customers.

A NEW RUSSIAN STYLE
Throughout the first half of the nineteenth

Below left: A forget-me-not spray, with flowers of blue enamel and rose-cut diamonds, standing in a rock-crystal vase ,which appears to contain water but is cut from a block of crystal in a trompe-l'oeil technique.

Below right: Cherries in carved purpurine, the blossoms enamelled opaque white with diamond centres.

Below left and right: A rabbit in purpurine (below left) and an elephant in nephrite (below right). Both animals show the influence of the Japanese netsuke carvings which greatly interested Fabergé, who had a large collection of them.

century there had been a vigourous philosophical debate in Russia between two schools of thought: the Westerners and the Slavophiles. The Westerners believed that Russia's future lay in aligning itself to Europe, while the Slavophiles wanted Russia to find its future in itself, in its own culture. One of the leaders of the Slavophile school, Peter Chaadayev, wrote in 1836: 'We are not of the West nor of the East and we have the traditions of neither'. This conflict was continued in the world of art. Those who followed the Old-Russian school called for an end to the slavish imitation of Western art and a return to Russian values, while those who looked to the West believed that doors should be opened to the European tradition.

Fabergé does not appear to have been closely associated with the Mir Iskvussa (World of Art) movement, which was a grouping of intellectuals founded in 1898 including such figures as Alexandre Benois, Sergei Diaghilev and Léon Bakst, who produced an influential magazine and had close links with artistic movements beyond Russia. They brought new vigour to all the arts – painting, ballet, music and literature. The Ballets Russes, centred on Diaghilev, was a direct result of their ideas, and they made known the works of such artists as Cézanne, Van Gogh and Matisse in Russia. They were also interested in the applied arts, promoting such exponents as Tiffany, Gallé and Colonna, and at an exhibition in 1906 the work of the Scottish designer Charles Rennie Mackintosh was exhibited.

The movement also sought to encourage folk crafts in Russia, but it was still overwhelmingly Western in its sympathies. As Alexandre Benois explained: 'We objected both to Russian coarseness and to the decorative complacency that many Russians love to parade'.

Although the young Benois and his fellow intellectuals were devoted to Russia, they reacted against some elements of their country. 'In Russia,' he said, 'much that was characteristically Russian annoyed us by its coarseness, triviality and unattractive barbarism.'

Yet there was nothing radical in the movement, its members being conservative, usually monarchist. Benois adds the surprising information that the journal *Mir Iskvussa* was saved

from extinction by a personal gift of 10,000 roubles from the tsar himself. Fabergé had some links with the movement from his association with Benois, who carried out designs for his firm; it is to him that the Imperial 'Colonnade Egg' of 1905 is attributed.

THE DEFINITIVE FABERGÉ STYLE

It is not clear how much Fabergé was affected by the Mir Iskvussa movement, but he was certainly fully aware of it and, typically, he used whatever aspects of the movement attracted him. He was, above all, Russian, and was therefore influenced by the culture of his own country.

As an individual and as a businessman, he was alert to changes of mood and fashion, and his work reflects a number of these changes during his lifetime. There are themes that are constant in his work: the quality of craftsmanship, the avoidance of embellishment and overstatement. Some of his work is indeed surprisingly modern in approach, years ahead of its time. The cigarette cases are an example, fashioned in beautiful materials but strictly functional. Stripped of excess ornamentation, they are miracles of craftsmanship, combining design and workmanship, and are in themselves a definition of good taste.

One of Fabergé's great contributions to the arts of goldsmithing, silversmithing and jewellery-making is in the use of colour. He drew on an unusually large range of colours in almost all his work, and colour was also an important consideration in his use of gold. It could be changed by mixing gold with other metals, which was also necessary to increase the hardness, because gold is basically a soft substance which wears easily. The addition of silver gives a green tinge to the original yellow, copper gives red gold and nickel makes white gold. More subtle effects are possible with the addition of other alloys to give blue-, orange- and grey-tinted golds, all of which can be seen in Fabergé's work at different times, though in general he favoured the more basic colours. He was particularly inspired by *or en quatre couleurs* (four-colour gold), which was widely used in eighteenth-century French snuffboxes. Fabergé used the technique widely, but it is probably seen at its best in the cigarette cases, where different shades of gold are juxtaposed to great effect. He also used different surfaces – ribbed, smooth, banded – to emphasise the different shades of colour and to add to the tactile pleasure of the object.

Further examples of Fabergé's use of different colours of gold can be seen in his decorative touches, such as garlands in which different shades are used to represent leaves and flowers – a technique used in a vast range of objects, from picture frames to Imperial Easter eggs. A novel effect used on some gold and silver objects was a rough, nugget-like

Below: Dress studs in gold and enamel set with diamonds.

Below left: A double-portrait brooch in which the gold and platinum miniatures of Nicholas II and Alexandra Feodorovna are set with circular-cut diamonds. The ribbon above is set with diamonds and decorated with a sapphire and a rose-cut diamond.

appearance obtained by using the *samordok* technique, in which the gold is heated to a certain point and then abruptly cooled, the drop in temperature affecting the surface.

FABERGÉ'S ENAMELLING

Perhaps what is most striking about Fabergé's workmanship is the quality of the enamelling, which was achieved by the lavish use of time and labour. Again, his inspiration was the work of French eighteenth-century craftsmen, and he both revived old techniques which had been lost and refined those techniques to achieve even more splendid results.

There are complicated technical problems associated with enamelling, particularly because it is carried out at very high temperatures. A compound of glass and metal oxides is heated until it begins to melt and is then applied and fused to a prepared metal surface, usually silver, which has been engraved. Fabergé was clearly fascinated by the possibilities of enamelling and exploited them to the full, with results that can be seen in a range of objects, most of them miniatures. He also created designs which involved the enamelling of larger surfaces, but then abandoned these efforts because of the difficulties involved. His craftsmen were also capable of enamelling rounded surfaces, a notoriously difficult exercise, using a technique known as *en ronde bosse*.

The depth of finish in Fabergé's enamelling

Left: The 'Colonnade Egg', by workmaster Henrik Wigström, presented by Nicholas II to his wife, the Empress Alexandra Feodorovna, in 1905. This is a romantic creation, a temple of love in bowenite surmounted by a silver-gilt cupid with four silver-gilt cherubs at the base. The clock's dial is set with rose-cut diamonds.

was achieved by layering several coats of enamel, as many as six, at decreasing temperatures. This was a delicate and highly skilled process, especially when the piece was not flat. The so-called 'oyster', opalescent effect seen in Fabergé's works was obtained by beginning with a semi-transparent layer of enamel in an orange shade and then applying a number of coats of clear enamel to achieve the much-prized and beautiful iridescent effect. Sometimes gold-leaf patterns, *paillons*, or paintings of flowers or trees, were inserted between the layers, a complicated process which involved the application of the additional material to a surface which had already been fired before adding the final, sealing layer. The visual effects were heightened by the decorations (often waves or sunbursts) engraved on the metal or *guilloche* surface. These designs could be carried out by hand, but were usually made with a machine called a *tour à guilloche*. The enamel was finally polished with a wooden wheel and chamois leather for many, many hours. This skilled and lengthy job was essential if the finish for which Fabergé enamel was renowned was to be achieved.

Below left: A gold and jewelled cigarette case, by the workmaster Henrik Wigström. The map represents Nicholas II's favourite resort in the Crimea. The Black Sea is set with calibré-*cut sapphires; the Crimean mountains are formed from textured gold; a line of* calibré-*cut rubies marks the road from Sebastopol to Yalta, with precious stones for towns. The railway is represented by emeralds.*

USE OF COLOUR IN ENAMELLING

The texture of the finished article, the all-important feel, was achieved by methods which typified both Fabergé's approach to his work and the period in which he lived, when the amount of time taken or the cost of the materials necessary to produce an object were not prime considerations.

Fabergé increased the use of colour in his enamelling and was always ready to experiment with new shades, drawing on a palette of 144 different basic colours. Typically, Fabergé used them in a wide range of objects, such as Imperial eggs, picture frames, parasol handles, miniature furniture, bell pushes, flowers, boxes, tie pins, cigarette cases, paper knives and much more. Each of these objects, however ordinary, was enamelled with the same degree of painstaking care.

Since there was no mark for enamellers, unlike goldsmiths and silversmiths, the superbly skilled craftsmen who carried out the delicate work were usually anonymous, but some of the Fabergé enamellers can take credit posthumously for their skills (which, according to Kenneth Snowman, required 'the combination of the gardener's green fingers and the touch of the successful pastry cook'). Fabergé's son, Eugène, identified Alexander Petrov, his son, Nicholas, and Vassili Boitzov for posterity.

CLOISONNÉ ENAMELLING

Fabergé also used *cloisonné* enamelling in the traditional Russian style to satisfy his more conservative customers. In this technique, small spaces or cells (*cloisons* in French) are formed with metal wires on a silver surface and are then filled with coloured enamel. The patterns formed are vivid in colour and traditional in style, with strong, floral designs. At one time this Russian style was considered

Above left: A two-coloured-gold cigarette case in the Renaissance revivalist style, with a sapphire push-button.

Above right: A cylindrical cigarette case once owned by the Grand Duchess Anastasia of Greece.

Far left: A silver, gold and enamel cigarette case.

Left: A guilloche-enamel and silver-gilt cigarette case.

too primitive for Western tastes, but in recent years there has been greater recognition of the vigour and authenticity of the work of such leading masters as Ovchinnikov, Semenova, Ruckert and Saltikov, and modern museums are delighted to be able to exhibit their works.

The Old-Russian style, which had its roots in the seventeenth century, enjoyed a revival in the nineteenth century with the development of the Pan-Slavic movement. At first, Fabergé sold the *cloisonné* work of other people, such as Maria Semenova, who employed about 100 people at her Moscow workshop, but later he engaged Fedor Ruckert, who was a master of the *cloisonné* technique and used it quite differently than his contemporaries. His designs were modern, even suggestive of Art Nouveau, and the colours he employed were more muted than those of enamellers such as Ovchinnikov. The difference is quite startling when the work of the two craftsmen is viewed side by side.

OTHER ENAMELLING TECHNIQUES

Champlevé enamelling was another method that Fabergé used. Here the enamel is used to fill a groove, after which it is made level with the surrounding area. He also used the technique of *plique à jour*, in which the enamel is not backed and the colour of each of the sections can be seen when the piece is held up to the light, giving a brilliant effect.

Enamelling techniques were used in much of the jewellery made in the Fabergé workshops, heightening the jewels' colour. Up to then, jewellery had tended to be rather ornate in style, emphasising the size and value of the precious stones used.

FABERGÉ JEWELLERY

Fabergé's approach was to use precious stones and materials as components of the design, choosing them for their suitability rather than their value. As a consequence, semi-precious stones, which other jewellers would have considered quite unsuitable, were often used. Favoured precious stones were emeralds, rubies and sapphires, which were usually *en cabochon* – polished but not faceted. Rose-

Below: An Imperial presentation brooch in gold-white guilloche enamel, diamonds and sapphires, shown with its original red morocco case, stamped with the double-headed eagle. The brooch was presented by Alexandra Feodorovna to her English nanny, Miss Jean Bolestone.

Below: This oval brooch has an enamel plaque painted with a winged Cupid in the style of François Boucher. The grey guilloche-enamel border is edged by two bands of rose-cut diamonds.

Bottom centre and bottom right: Beautiful examples of the workmanship of Fabergé's craftsmen. The frame in the centre is in the Rococo style, with superb guilloche enamelling, and the one on the right is sumptuously embellished in gold.

cut diamonds were preferred to brilliant-cut diamonds, because the rose-cut diamond, in which the top is cut in triangular facets, is less obtrusive than the brilliant.

Of course, as a jeweller to the Imperial court, Fabergé was often called upon to provide sumptuous pieces. For example, there was the superb creation of pearls presented by Alexander III to the young Alexandra of Hesse when she became engaged to his son, Nicholas. It was said to be worth 250,000 roubles and was described by Agathon Fabergé as the biggest single transaction his father ever had with the tsars.

The House of Fabergé also held in stock a selection of major pieces of jewellery – necklaces, tiaras and so on – for rich patrons in Russia and abroad. Many of these pieces have

disappeared, because they were broken up and sold by Russian émigrés in the years after the revolution, and this explains why Fabergé's output of pure jewellery is not as well represented in modern collections as are other examples of his work.

USE OF STONES IN FABERGÉ JEWELLERY

More typical of Fabergé's work as a jeweller are the small, relatively modest pieces, such as brooches and pendants, cufflinks, bracelets and the miniature Easter eggs for which his firm was famous. These were given at Easter and were made up into necklaces, added to year by year. The miniature eggs, less than 25mm (1in) high, are marvellous examples of craftsmanship; often in brightly coloured enamel, they are decorated with precious or

semi-precious stones in a variety of designs, frequently celebrating a special date or commemorating a regiment; or they are decorated with flowers and animals, and are sometimes made of superbly polished hardstones, such as bowenite, rose quartz and chalcedony. These miniature marvels were popular in Russia for the traditional Easter rituals and also found favour in the more sophisticated world of Edwardian society, as shown in the account books of Fabergé's London branch.

From his work, it seems that Fabergé preferred stones of great beauty and modest value, often from Russia's own resources, but also from the rest of the world. The choice of such stones brought a new dimension to the work of the craftsman-jeweller, making available subtle new colours and textures.

THE FABERGÉ HALLMARK

There was nothing conservative about the designer's choice of materials. Anything was possible in the search for new effects for the flood of designs necessary to meet the huge demand for Fabergé's work. Steel was used for the blue globe which was part of the Imperial Easter egg of 1913, made to celebrate the tercentenary of Romanov rule. A daring touch in the creation of a dandelion at the point of seeding was to use strands of asbestos fibre for the puff of seeds. Again,

This page: Fabergé created extraordinarily beautiful handles for a wide range of objects, in all manner of designs and in all kinds of stones, such as nephrite and bowenite, often with guilloche *enamelling. Some delightful examples are shown on this page: a table seal (above), a parasol handle (lar left) and a parasol handle (left) with a pair of chalk-holders.*

obtaining the desired effect was more important than the value of the materials.

Presiding over the choice of materials was the patriarchal figure of Fabergé himself. It was his influence, in person or in spirit, which moulded the whole of the Fabergé empire's output, just as it was his eye that examined each item produced by the firm and judged whether it should carry the Fabergé hallmark or not. If he decided that it should not (and there were many times when objects were rejected), the offending article was dismantled and sent back to the workshops. There were no appeals, no arguments. In this matter Fabergé was an artistic despot who did not feel the need to explain himself. Bainbridge has recorded in detail how he would simply reject a piece, seemingly faultless, without comment, because it contained some flaw visible to him alone.

Left: Fabergé's enamelwork is famous for its quality, revealed here in the beautiful deep blue of the egg-shaped handle of this desk seal, crowned by a replica of the emblem of the Chevalier's Guard Regiment, and in the miniature Easter eggs which surround it, which were extremely popular as gifts.

THE FABERGÉ EGGS:

UN GÉNIE INCOMPARABLE

Previous page: The 'Lilies-of-the-valley Egg', workmaster Michael Perchin, presented by Nicholas II to his mother in 1898 (15cm/5¹⁵⁄₁₆in open). Its surprise is three miniature portraits of the tsar and the Grand duchesses Olga and Tatiana.

Below: The 'Alexander III Equestrian Egg', signed by Fabergé, presented by Tsar Nicholas II to his mother, the dowager empress, in 1910 (15.5cm/6⅛in). The shell is made of rock crystal mounted on platinum, and inside is a gold statue of Alexander III on horseback.

Fabergé's fame rests on his achievement in creating the series of Imperial eggs – the result of an act of patronage on a grand scale by the Imperial family of Russia. The commission gave Fabergé the freedom to ignore questions of cost and time and to concentrate on the challenge of creating something new and spectacular each year, a challenge he met with outstanding success, as can be seen in the extraordinary examples of craftsmanship and imagination described and illustrated in these pages.

The Imperial eggs, which have been seen by so many and are guaranteed to attract vast crowds wherever they are exhibited, were never intended to be seen by the public at large. Their creation and presentation were private matters between patron and artist. Indeed, secrecy surrounded the creation of each egg at all stages. Bainbridge has recalled how he discovered the existence of these extraordinary works quite by accident in the St Petersburg offices one morning, when he saw Henrik Wigström carrying 'something the like of which I had never seen before'. The Englishman went on:

> There was I, admitted to every intimacy by the head of the house and his family, with carte blanche *to roam where I liked and do what I liked on the business premises, ask questions of anybody, and open any drawers that took my fancy, and yet but for this chance happening I should have remained ignorant of the finest objects the House was all the time producing.*

THE FIRST COMMISSION

There is some doubt about how the first commission came about. One story is that the eggs were a speculative creation by Fabergé in an effort to win the favour of the tsar. Another is that they were an attempt by Alexander III to relieve the grief of his wife, Marie Feodorovna, after the assassination of Alexander II in 1881. The most popular story, however, is that they were a sentimental gesture on his part to remind the empress of her Danish home, a commission for which Fabergé had the happy idea of recreating a jewelled and enamelled gold Easter egg which was in the possession of the Danish royal family.

Whatever the circumstances were, the first Imperial Easter egg was so well received that Alexander III ordered that a similar work should be created each year for his wife. The commission was continued by his son, who increased it to two: one for his mother and one for his wife.

The series of Imperial Easter eggs is a spectacular achievement, recalling the works of art created by artists and craftsmen for the great princes of the Renaissance. Cost was not a consideration, and the precious materials used were the least important part of the creation. The craftsman's contribution was inspiration: what mattered most was that the piece should be new and surprising. If Fabergé had unusual freedom because of the nature of the commission, he also had the responsibility of finding something novel to delight his Imperial patrons. With the help of his team of designers and craftsmen, he succeeded magnificently, creating more than 50 works of art, extraordinary examples of ingenuity, craftsmanship and imagination.

There has been some uncertainty about the date of the first Imperial egg, but recent research in Russia, by Marina Lopato of the Hermitage Museum, St Petersburg, has established that it was 1885 (the commission continued until 1917).

ORIGINS OF THE IMPERIAL EGGS
It was appropriate that Alexander III, the most Russian of tsars, should have chosen to present his empress with an egg at Easter. The exchanging of eggs at this time of year was a popular custom in Russia then, as it is today. In earlier times, these symbolic Easter offerings were natural eggs, painted in simple colours, but they began to become more exotic in the eighteenth century, probably influenced by the appearance of expensive, jewelled eggs in Western Europe. They were made of a variety of materials, such as wood, *papier-mâché* and porcelain, beautifully crafted and

Below: The 'Twelve-monogram Egg', workmaster Michael Perchin, presented by Tsar Alexander III to his wife, the Empress Marie Feodorovna, probably in 1892. Made of gold, it has six guilloche *panels in which the monograms of the tsar and his wife, MF and A III, are set in rose-cut diamonds, with a large diamond above and below. It is believed that the piece marked their silver wedding anniversary in 1892.*

Below: The 'Easter Egg with Twelve Panels', workmaster Michael Perchin, was a gift to Barbara Kelch from her husband in 1899 (8.9cm/3½in). It is enamelled in pale, translucent pink and has 12 panels, each with a violet-painted motif. The dividing bands are of enamelled roses and leaves. Barbara Kelch's initials are under a diamond on the top.

highly prized, sometimes enamelled and jewelled. Miniature eggs in the form of pendants appeared in the eighteenth century, and examples must have been known to Fabergé, who made a speciality of producing a range of these enchanting objects in a variety of materials and decorations and in a staggering number of designs, barely repeating himself. They were collected by the wives and daughters of wealthy families and were worn as chains; some linked as many as 100 of the tiny objects and admirers would add others to mark different occasions.

'Surprise' eggs appeared in eighteenth-century France, in the reign of Louis XVI, who had the charming habit of hiding a

precious object in an egg, which he would press on some favourite at Easter. An unusual example of the surprise element of these eggs is a gift given by the king to his aunt, Madame Victoire, of two eggs which contain dramatic scenes illustrating a real-life story of a young girl being attacked by robbers, being saved by soldiers and being returned in safety to her home. The miniature world – the eggs are not more than 5cm (2in) in diameter – by an unknown hand are beautifully made, with figures of wax and foliage of silk and velvet.

During this period, extravagant Easter eggs were exchanged by royalty and the aristocracy. These were the magnificent creations of the French goldsmiths of the eighteenth

century to whom Fabergé was indebted. There are numerous examples in the Louvre in Paris, exquisite works, beautifully crafted in precious stones and materials.

There were richly wrought eggs made in other countries, too, especially Germany and Austria, and the Hermitage Museum in St Petersburg has a number of treasures of this kind from the eighteenth century which would have been known to Fabergé.

THE NUMBER OF IMPERIAL EGGS

There has been some uncertainty about the number of Imperial Easter eggs produced by Fabergé, and there are doubts as to the dating of some of them. This reflects the private nature of the commissions. In other words, they were not regarded as lavish works of art to be talked about and admired on the public stage but were family gifts, precious and highly imaginative but also simple, personal tokens of affection.

From the first Imperial egg of 1885, Fabergé presented Alexander III with a further creation each year until the tsar's death in 1894. His son, Nicholas II, then continued the custom. So 10 eggs were made during the reign of Alexander III and a further 44 during the reign of Nicholas II, making a total of 54 eggs (or 56, if the Imperial eggs for the fateful year of 1917 are included, although they are now lost and there is no evidence that they were ever delivered).

Research in Russia has suggested that more Imperial Easter eggs than the 10 of Alexander III's reign were made by Fabergé. Fabergé scholar Geza von Habsburg has speculated that these may have been gifts to the tsarevitch.

Whatever the difficulties of establishing dates for the creation of the Imperial eggs, we know that 47 of the original 54 (or 56) exist today. The Armoury Museum of the Kremlin has 10, but many of the others have passed through several hands since the revolution. America has the richest collection – the inveterate and persistent collector Malcolm Forbes acquired no less than 11 of these now priceless objects during his lifetime. Eight are in European collections and some are lost. It is

Below: The 'Imperial Rosebud Egg', in red guilloche enamel, workmaster Michael Perchin, presented by Tsar Nicholas II to his wife, Alexandra Feodorovna, in 1895. The surprise is a rosebud, in yellow and green enamel, which contains a diamond- and ruby-set crown.

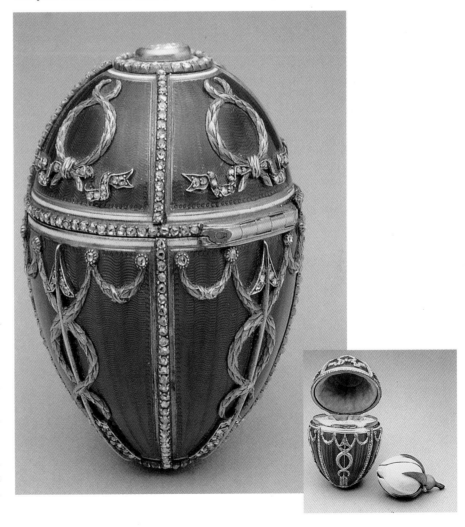

Below right: The 'Hoof Egg', workmaster Michael Perchin, is thought to have been presented by the Empress Alexandra to one of her friends. The bowenite shell stands on four cloven-hooved legs and is decorated with gold laurel pendants and swags with diamond-set, ruby bows. The surprise is a gold-framed miniature of the empress wearing the Kokoshnik *diadem.*

Below left: The 'Grisaille Egg' (also known as the 'Catherine the Great Egg', workmaster Henrik Wigström, has eight grisaille panels, enamelled translucent pink, edged by narrow, white-enamel bands and pearl borders. The paintings, by Vassily Zuiev, represent the Muses. The surprise inside the 'Grisaille Egg', presented by Nicholas II to the Dowager Empress Marie Feodorovna in 1914, is a tiny sedan chair containing a figure of Catherine the Great, carried by two black servants who walk when the mechanism is wound.

known that some owners are reluctant, given the value of the Imperial eggs, to admit that they own them.

UN GÉNIE INCOMPARABLE

A surprise was the essential element of the Imperial Easter gifts; this helps to explain the secrecy surrounding their creation. When the tsar asked to be allowed some details of the forthcoming gift, even he was denied by Fabergé,

with the words 'Your Majesty will be content'.

Fabergé made the delivery of each Easter gift personally to the tsar, and later, when there were two eggs to be delivered, the duty was undertaken by one of his sons. It was obviously a ceremony that everyone looked forward to, the Imperial family being eager to see what masterpiece the craftsman had created, the craftsman anxious for approval.

Alexander von Solodkoff, in his book

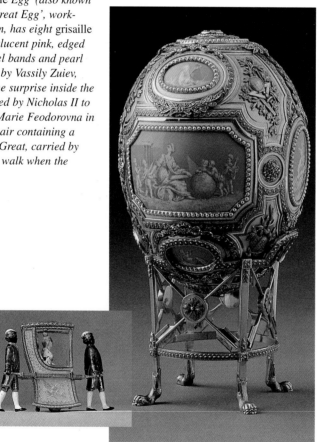

Fabergé, has described the approval of the Dowager Empress Marie Feodorovna of the Easter egg given to her by her son in 1914:

> *Fabergé brought it to me himself. It is a true chef-d'oeuvre, in pink enamel and inside a porte-chaise carried by two negroes with Empress Catherine in it . . . You wind it up and then the negroes walk – it is an unbelivably beautiful and superbly fine piece of work. Fabergé is the greatest genius of our time. I also told him: 'Vous êtes un génie incomparable'.*

Her enthusiasm, lively and infectious, had been expressed many times at these Easter ceremonies, for the 1914 presentation was the twenty-ninth year that Fabergé had created a masterpiece for her. The workmaster for the dowager empress' Easter gift was Henrik Wigström, and it is a superb example of his work, made of gold, decorated with eight *grisaille* panels, and translucent pink, set within pearl borders and white-enamel bands, with each panel depicting one of the Muses, painted by Vassily Zuiev. Known as the *'Grisaille Egg'*, or *'Catherine the Great Egg'*, it is now in the Marjorie Merriweather Post Collection at Hillwood Musuem, Washington, DC.

Eugene Fabergé has described how he travelled across Russia, from St Petersburg to Sebastopol, to deliver the 1912 Easter gift for the Empress Alexandra, being driven to the tsar's palace at Livadia for an audience with Nicholas II, who expressed his satisfaction with the egg. Known as the 'Tsarevitch Egg', it

Below left: The 'Chanticleer Egg', workmaster Michael Perchin, presented to Barbara Kelch, probably in 1904. The shell, and the four panels of the base, are enamelled a brilliant sapphire blue on a guilloche ground. Gold swags hang from the grille at the top, from which a colourful cockerel emerges to crow.

Below: The 'Renaissance Egg', workmaster Michael Perchin, presented by Tsar Alexander III to his wife, the Empress Marie Feodorovna, in 1894 (13.3cm/5¼in long). This sumptuous object is in grey agate, encased in a trellis of white enamel and rose-cut diamonds. The date is set in diamonds on a red guilloche emblem. Carved heads of lions with rings in their mouths act as handles. The inspiration for the piece is an almost identical work by Le Roy, dating from the early eighteenth century, in the Green Vaults at Dresden.

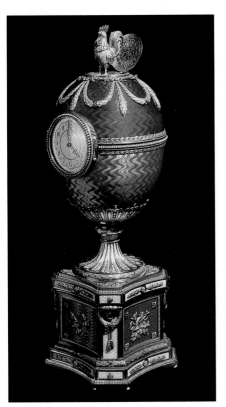

Below: The 'Resurrection Egg', workmaster Michael Perchin, presented by Alexander III to his wife (9.8cm/3⁷⁄₈in).

Right: The 'Cross of St George Egg', signed 'Fabergé', presented by Nicholas II to his mother, the dowager empress, in 1916 (8.4cm/3⁵⁄₁₆in). In recognition of the need for economy because of the war, the shell is made of silver, enamelled opalescent white. The crosses of St George spring up when a button is pressed, revealing miniatures of Nicholas II (as shown) and his son, Alexis.

contained the Russian double-headed eagle in diamonds framing a portrait of the Tsarevitch Alexis. The egg itself is carved from a solid block of lapis lazuli, elaborately decorated with gold motifs of flowers, cherubs and scrolls. The egg is now in the Lilian Thomas Pratt Collection, Virginia Museum of Fine Arts, Richmond, Virginia.

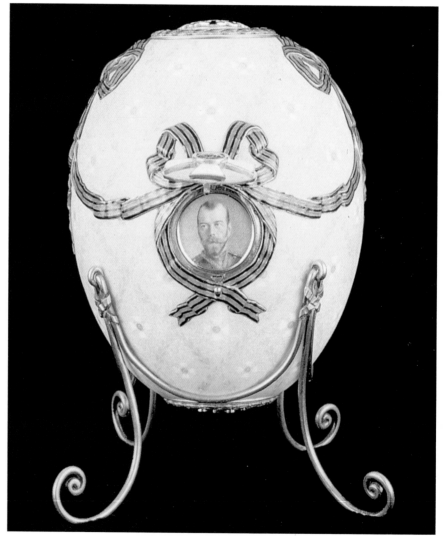

THE EARLY IMPERIAL EGGS

Most of the early Imperial eggs are derivative, drawing on the styles of the past, much as the rest of Fabergé's early work had done. The inspiration for the first egg, the 'Hen Egg' (or 'First Imperial Egg') of 1885, as has been mentioned, was clearly designs of the same kind, especially the golden egg in the Danish Royal Collection. The 'Renaissance Egg', dated 1894, is a sumptuous object in grey agate, with white enamel bands set with quatrefoils of rose-cut diamonds with ruby centres where the bands cross; on the top is a red *guilloche*-enamel plaque on which the date 1894 is set in rose-cut diamonds; around the sides are brilliant red, green and blue enamelled Renaissance motifs set with diamonds and cabochon rubies. The inspiration for this object was a jewelled casket made by the goldsmith Le Roy, which was in the Green Vaults Collection at Dresden and which would have been known to Fabergé from his student days there. Although it is virtually the same, it is not a perfect copy, as the shape is slightly different, Fabergé's casket being more egg shaped. This fact has led some scholars to suppose that Fabergé's inspiration came not from Le Roy's work itself but from a colour print of the original. Both works can be seen and compared – Fabergé's is in the Forbes Collection, New York, and Le Roy's is still in the Green Vaults Collection. The original surprise, probably a large jewel, has been lost, a fate which befell many of the surprises of the Imperial eggs. The surprise in the 'Blue-enamel Ribbed Egg', dated 1887 or 1890, has also been lost. This beautifully enamelled work, in royal-blue *guilloche* enamel, is thought to have been inspired by four vodka cups in the form of Easter eggs in the Hermitage Museum.

The 'Resurrection Egg' is evidently influenced by the Italian Renaissance and may well have been inspired by a particular piece. It is a fantastic creation: the base is richly enamelled in the Renaissance style; above it sits a large, natural pearl, and poised above that is a carved egg of rock crystal, which contains a scene from the Resurrection. Although modern scholars are unsure of the date of the piece, it is now thought to have been the second Imperial egg given by Alexander III to his wife. It is, incidentally, one of only two in the entire series of Fabergé's Imperial eggs to make any direct reference to the religious significance of Easter, which is a little surprising because

Below: The beautiful 'Mosaic Egg' was presented by Tsar Nicholas II to his wife, Alexandra Feodorovna, in 1914 (9.2cm/3⅝in). The complicated pattern is made up of rubies, emeralds, diamonds, garnets, sapphires and topazes, bordered with pearls. It opens to reveal a surprise of a bejewelled gold frame on a pedestal, containing cameos of the five Imperial children painted on a pink-enamel background. It was designed by Alma Theresia Pihl in the workshops of Albert Holmström and is said to have been inspired by petit-point *embroidery.*

Below: The Imperial Easter egg of 1891, which was given by Alexander III to the Empress Marie Feodorovna (9.8cm/3⅞in). The jasper shell, with Rococo scrolls, opened to reveal a gold and platinum model of the cruiser Pamiat Azova, *in which Nicholas II made a world cruise before he became tsar.*

Empress Alexandra Feodorovna was intensely, perhaps obsessively, religious. The Russian people of the period were also greatly influenced by the Orthodox Church, and there was a lively trade in eggs bearing the words *Kristos voskresy* ('Christ is risen'), some with hand-painted icons inside.

THE COMMEMORATIVE EGGS

Many of the surprises have family associations: the 'Silver-anniversary Egg', or 'Twelve-monogram Egg', probably from 1892, features the monograms of Alexander III and his wife in rose-cut diamonds; the surprise of the 'Lilies-of-the-valley Egg' of 1898 is three miniatures of Nicholas and the Grand duchesses Olga and Tatiana; Alexander III is commemorated in the Imperial eggs of

1904; celebrated Romanov rulers in the 'Romanov Tercentenary Egg' of 1913; and the 'Mosaic Egg' of 1914, the design of which is said to have been inspired by *petit-point* embroidery, has a surprise of a miniature frame with portraits of the five Imperial children. Some referred to Imperial residences: the Imperial egg of 1901 contained a replica, beautifully executed, of the Gatchina Palace, a favourite of the dowager empress; that of 1895 for the dowager had a surprise of a screen of 10 panels showing Danish and Russian palaces and the Imperial yachts. Some commemorate special events: the surprise of the Imperial egg of 1891 was the model of the cruiser *Pamiat Azova*, on which Nicholas II had made his world cruise while still tsarevitch; an equally accurate representation,

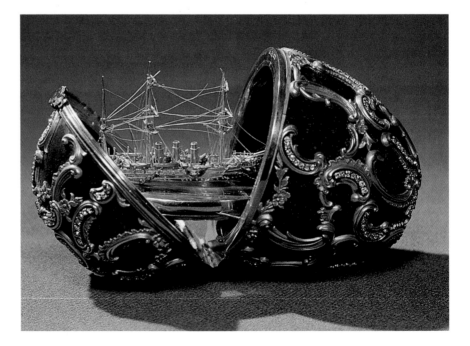

faithful in every detail, is the surprise of the Imperial egg of 1900, the year the Trans-Siberian Railway was inaugurated, which has a clockwork model of the Trans-Siberian express, exquisitely made with diamonds for the front lights and rubies for the rear lights.

The finest of the commemorative eggs – for some, the greatest achievement of Fabergé – is undoubtedly the 'Coronation Egg' of 1897, which was presented by Nicholas II to Empress Alexandra at the first Easter after the coronation. It is probably the most famous of the Fabergé eggs, a sumptuous creation, rich in materials and style, a fitting memorial to the powerful Romanov dynasty. The workmaster was Michael Perchin, the

genius who became Fabergé's head workmaster at St Petersburg at the age of 26 and who was responsible for the glittering series of Imperial eggs from then until his death in 1903. The colour scheme is based on the coronation robes of Nicholas II: gold, with panels of translucent primrose enamel over *guilloche* sunray patterns, it has trelliswork of laurel bands with black-enamel Imperial eagles, each set with a rose-cut diamond at the points where the laurel bands cross. On the top is the monogram of the empress in rose-cut diamonds and cabochon rubies. Exquisite as this is, it is followed by an enchanting surprise: a perfect miniature of the coronation coach. The velvet upholstery of the original is reproduced in red enamel, the gilt-wood frame in chased gold and the glass windows in rock crystal; the interior is enamelled in powder blue for the curtains and turquoise for the ceiling, and

Below left and bottom: The 'Coronation Egg', presented by Tsar Nicholas II to his wife, the Empress Alexandra Feodorovna, in 1897 (12.7cm/5in), is regarded by some as Fabergé's greatest achievement.

Below centre and right: The 'Spring-flowers Egg', presented by Tsar Alexander III to his wife in 1890. The gold shell is enamelled translucent strawberry on a guilloche ground and is decorated with gold in the style of Louis XV. The surprise is charming: a bouquet of wood anemones, with white chalcedony petals, garnet centres and green-enamelled leaves, in a basket of platinum set with rose-cut diamonds.

*Below right: The 'Cuckoo-clock Egg',
workmaster Michael Perchin, presented by
Tsar Nicholas II to his mother, the Dowager
Empress Marie Feodorovna, in 1900
(20.6cm/8⅛in). The shell is a beautiful
shade of violet, enamelled on a* guilloche
*ground, supported by three slender
columns. When a button is depressed at the
back of the clock, a gold grille opens and
a bird (not a cuckoo but a cockerel)
appears, crowing and moving
its wings.*

*Opposite page: The 'Red Cross Egg
with Resurrection Triptych',
workmaster Henrik Wigström,
presented by Tsar Nicholas II to his
wife, the Empress Alexandra, in
1915 (8.5cm/3⅜in). The shell is of
white transparent enamel, with
crosses in red enamel. In the centre
of the crosses at the front and back
are miniatures of two of the tsar's
children, the Grand duchesses Olga
and Tatiana. The egg opens to
reveal a triptych.*

above the coach is an Imperial crown in rose-cut diamonds. It is a perfect copy in every way, even down to the steps, which are let down when the doors are opened. This degree of fidelity was achieved with extraordinary care and great patience, as always with Fabergé's masterpieces. It was modelled by George Stein, a former coachmaker turned goldsmith, who spent 15 months on the task

under the direction of Perchin and his then assistant, Wigström (Wigström's daughter remembered going with her father to the Imperial stables to check on the exact colours of the interior of the coach).

OBJECTS OF FANTASY
For some, the most pleasing of Fabergé's Imperial eggs are those which are not linked to people, places or events but which are truly objects of fantasy, having no point other than to give pleasure. The 'Spring-flowers Egg', possibly from 1890, is a delight: the gold shell is enamelled a deep, strawberry red on a *guilloche* pattern, and the whole shape is encased in Rococo goldwork in the Louis XV style, opening to reveal a basket of spring flowers which have white chalcedony petals with garnets, engraved gold stems and petals in enamelled translucent green. The 'Clover-leaf Egg' of 1902 continues the theme of nature, the inspiration of Art Nouveau: the shell of clover leaves is in green enamel, a deceptively simple, stunning design.

Mechanical surprises were featured in a number of the Fabergé Imperial eggs, and it is possible that Fabergé's interest in mechanical toys was kindled by his old mentor, Peter Hiskias Pendin, who had acted as friend and adviser when the young Fabergé took over his father's business in 1870. Pendin had been trained as an optician, a not uncommon background for makers of automata, as a number of gifted Swiss craftsmen of the nineteenth century had originally been opticians.

The 'Cuckoo-clock Egg' of 1900, a richly ornate creation in the Baroque style, had a bird surprise. When a button is pressed at the back of the clock, a gold grille on the

*Right: The 'Duchess of Marlborough Egg',
workmaster Michael Perchin, made for
Consuelo, Duchess of Marlborough, in
1902. The duchess was American, a
member of the extremely wealthy Vanderbilt
family. The egg is almost identical to the
'Imperial Serpent Clock Egg', presented by
Tsar Alexander III to his wife, the Empress
Marie Feodorovna, in 1889, except that the
duchess' egg is pink rather than blue.*

top rises and the bird – not a cuckoo but a cockerel, as it happens – appears, resplendent with natural feathers, gold legs and cabochon-ruby eyes. The beak and wings move as the bird crows and then descends into the clock.

The 'Peacock Egg', dated 1908, also has a sophisticated mechanical surprise: a superb gold and enamelled peacock, which can be seen inside a rock-crystal egg within the branches of a gold tree, which has flowers of precious stones. The peacock can be taken from its perch and wound up to make it strut in an authentic fashion, moving its head and proudly displaying its magnificent tail in various colours of enamel. The bird is said to have been a copy of a peacock automaton, made by James Cox, in the Hermitage Museum. Such sophisticated mechanisms took considerable time to make and refine: the 'Peacock Egg' took workmaster Dorofeiiev three years to complete, beginning with a life-sized model and gradually reducing it to the necessary miniature scale.

THE END OF AN ERA

The bold flights of imagination and the lavish use of materials ended with the arrival of the war in 1914. Such exotic objects, inspired by the desire to give pleasure regardless of cost, had no place in a country suffering terrible losses through war. The two eggs of 1915 have a more sombre style. The eggs presented to the Empress Alexandra and the dowager empress by Nicholas II both feature Red Cross motifs and are worlds away from the flamboyant days of the past. Their seriousness is appropriate for the time, reflecting two of the deep interests of the Empress Alexandra Feodorovna: the Church and the Red Cross.

It has to be said that solemnity and seriousness are not ideal qualities for the creation of an *objet de fantasie*. The 'Steel Military Egg' of 1916 is a depressing object, made of steel in recognition of the war effort and standing on four miniature shells on a nephrite base. Inside the egg is a small easel supporting a gold frame which had a miniature painting by Zuiev of Nicholas II and his son with the generals at the front. The two final Imperial eggs, said to have been made of karelian birch and lapis lazuli respectively, are lost and may never have been delivered as the tsar's family moved towards its tragic and violent end.

Although the eggs are Fabergé's greatest achievement for the Imperial family, he also provided beautiful examples for a few favoured patrons, some of which were near-copies of

Below: The 'Peacock Egg', workmaster Henrik Wigström, presented by Tsar Nicholas II to his mother, the dowager empress, in 1908 (15.2cm/6in). Inside the rock-crystal egg is a gold and enamelled peacock which can be taken out and wound up so that it struts to and fro, moving its head and displaying its splendid tail.

the Imperial eggs. These patrons included Emanuel Nobel, the Duchess of Marlborough and the fabulously rich Siberian gold magnate Alexander Kelch, who commissioned seven eggs for his wife, Barbara, between 1898 and 1904. Among the eggs made for the Kelches are the fantastic, blue-enamelled 'Chanticleer Egg' and the equally lavish 'Pine-cone Egg'.

THE IMPERIAL EGGS: A UNIQUE ACHIEVEMENT

The Imperial eggs are a truly remarkable achievement and it is difficult to imagine anyone making them in today's conditions, which may explain why the modern world is so fascinated by them. For more than 30 years Fabergé had the annual challenge of creating some new delight unhindered by considerations of cost, free to draw on any source, to use any material and every skill, to expend as many hours as necessary, to produce something the only purpose of which was to bring pleasure, creating a moment of delighted surprise on Easter morning.

It should be remembered, too, that these objects, which required so much effort to create and which loom so large in the imagination, were often miniatures. The first Imperial egg of 1885 is only 6.3cm (2½in) wide; the 'Coronation Egg' of 1897, with its surprise of a fabulous coach, is a mere 12.7cm (5in) high; and even the more lavish eggs which came later rarely exceeded 25cm (10in) – the largest by quite a margin is the 'Uspensky Cathedral Egg' of 1904 – 35cm (14in) high.

Left, below left and right: The splendid 'Pine-cone Egg', workmaster Michael Perchin, given by Alexander Kelch to his wife, Barbara, in 1900. The body is of a magnificent, translucent, royal-blue enamel over a sunburst guilloche *ground, encrusted with rose-cut diamond crescents. At the top, four diamonds form a quatrefoil enclosing the date, 1900. The surprise is as magnificent as the egg – an elephant automaton in oxidised silver carrying an enamelled mahout seated upon a gold-fringed red and green* guilloche-enamel *saddlecloth. When wound with a golden key, the elephant lumbers forward swishing its tail.*

THE STYLE FABERGÉ

Although the Imperial eggs are certainly the best-known examples of Fabergé's craftsmanship, many other items were produced in his workshops. At its zenith, the Fabergé operation employed some 500 people at its various branches and had patrons in Russia, Europe, the United States and the Far East. Thousands of items were produced to meet the almost insatiable demand for items carrying the famous name but, despite these demands, Fabergé insisted that each article produced by the firm should display identical high standard of materials and workmanship. Not everything produced by the House of Fabergé met with universal critical approval, but his pieces were always popular, and the unvarying quality of the craftmanship cannot be disputed.

FABERGÉ FLOWERS

For many people, Fabergé's greatest achievement as a goldsmith and jeweller was not the fabulous Imperial Easter eggs but the artificial flowers, which are so different from the

Previous page and right: An exquisite study, in which buttercups and cornflowers share the same stem (22.8cm/9in). The cornflower petals are enamelled in blue, translucent enamel, with diamond centres, and the buttercups have yellow guilloche *petals and rose-cut-diamond centres. The bee on one of the buttercup flowers is made from rose-cut diamonds with ruby eyes (detail right).*

Imperial creations. Whereas the eggs are the result of flights of imagination and technical ingenuity, the flowers are simple studies from nature, executed in precious materials.

Flowers in spring have a special significance in Russia, with its long, bitter, seemingly endless winters. In the heyday of the Romanovs, flowers were brought by train to St Petersburg from abroad to adorn the Imperial palaces. In 1922 Lili Dehn, who had been a great favourite of Empress Alexandra, recalled from her home in England (to where she and her Swedish husband had escaped after the revolution): 'In springtime and winter the air was fragrant with masses of lilac and lilies of the valley, which were sent daily from the Riviera'.

The empress was particularly fond of lilies, magnolias, wistaria, rhododendrons and violets, and, of these, lilies of the valley were her special favourites. It was therefore appropriate that the first flower study known to have been created by Fabergé should have been a basket of lilies of the valley presented to the empress in 1896 at her coronation.

Although they are painstakingly accurate

in most cases, Fabergé's flowers are not simply botanical specimens in precious materials. Sometimes the rules of nature are ignored: a cornflower may grow from the same stem as a buttercup and a sprig of wild cherry may display both blossom and fruit. In these cases, Fabergé was attempting to express the essence of the plants, and, once again, his choice of materials depended on their suitability for his purpose rather than their intrinsic value.

The work involved in these flower studies is so delicate that it is best studied with the help of a microscope. The leaves are made of paper-thin slices of nephrite (or, just occasionally, gold) and the veins on the surface are repeated on the back. The golden stems are engraved with tiny lines.

INSPIRATION FOR THE FABERGÉ FLOWERS

Fabergé's inspiration for the flower studies probably came from the magnificent flower arrangements in precious stones which were made in the eighteenth century. There are several examples in European museums, and three in the Hermitage Museum, which would have been known to him. They are more exotic, less naturalistic, than those he made, but the relationship is clear. A jewelled bouquet in the Hermitage has flowers and leaves of diamonds, emeralds, topazes, garnets and corals. It is the work of Jérémie Pauzie (1716–79), who was born in Geneva and opened a workshop in St Petersburg in 1740, working as a court jeweller until 1764.

Typically, Fabergé did not draw his inspiration from a single source. There does seem

Right: Pansies, with enamelled petals, diamond centres and nephrite leaves, appear to have been set in a vase of water, which is, in fact, solid rock crystal.

Below right: The catkins are formed from spun green gold in the study on the left, while white quartz has been used for the mock-orange flowers in the centre and rhodonite for the flowers of the bleeding heart on the right.

to be a connection with similar Chinese works of the late eighteenth century, studies which aim for a more naturalistic effect, especially in the carving of the nephrite leaves. The Japanese art of flower-arranging, *ikebana,* is also seen as an influence on a number of the flower studies. Alexander von Solodkoff, in his work on Fabergé, points to flowers in the Japanese style described in the ledgers of

Fabergé's London branch for 1907–8, particularly a Japanese pine, a Japanese cherry and a Japanese flower in bamboo. He adds that the rarity of the flower studies is demonstrated by the fact that only 35 were sold by the London branch in the period from 1907 to 1917, a time when some 10,000 items in total were sold. The types of flower are diverse, including pansies, cherries, daisies, roses,

violets, jasmine, daffodils, bluebells, crocuses and sweet peas, but not, curiously, the lilies of the valley which were so popular in Russia.

Given the popularity of the flower pieces, it is a little surprising that only 60 genuine examples are known to exist today. It may be that many of these delicate objects have not survived; it may be that there are more that have yet to be discovered, perhaps in the former Soviet Union. Examples of the flower studies can be seen in collections throughout the world: Queen Elizabeth II has a major collection of 20 and there are several others in leading American museums.

FUNCTIONAL OBJECTS
The flowers and the Imperial eggs are quite different expressions of Fabergé's art, but both

Below left: A gift for a lady's dressing table, the 'Balletta Box' was presented by Grand Duke Alexei Alexandrovitch to the ballerina Madame Elizabeth Balletta of the Imperial Michael Theatre, St Petersburg – a lady who had many admirers. It is a vanity case in gold and blue enamel decorated with trellis-work and containing a gold pencil, mirror, lipstick tube and compartments for powder.

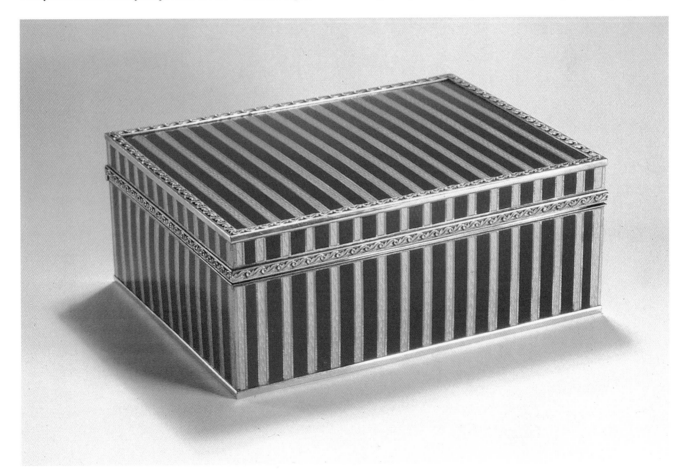

*Right: This nephrite and gold Imperial
presentation cigarette case was given
by Tsar Nicholas II to Kaiser Wilhelm
of Germany, and bears the German
emperor's monogram.*

share the distinction of being superb expressions of his creative genius. More typical of the works produced by Fabergé are the functional objects, a vast range of items produced in the St Petersburg workshops to cater for almost every domestic need: parasol and walking-stick handles, scent bottles, crochet hooks, letter-openers, glue pots, stampdampers, ashtrays, cigarette cases, boxes of all kinds, desk sets, clocks, photograph frames, electric bell pushes, snuffboxes, lorgnettes, opera glasses, thermometers, barometers and more. What is extraordinary about these things is not their diversity but the care which was lavished on each one of them. A crochet hook is made with the same degree of craftsmanship as something vastly more extravagant, carved in nephrite, one end embellished with white enamel on a *guilloche* ground and edged with a rose-cut-diamond border. A glue pot is made in bowenite, shaped like an over-ripe pear, complete with dark spots and a golden worm, the brush enamelled green and brown and set with a diamond. It is this devotion to quality that distinguishes the objects made by Fabergé from similar objects of today.

A fine example is the 'Balletta Box', a delightful vanity case in gold and blue enamel with a trelliswork of rose-cut diamonds and the monogram 'EB', the initials of the owner, the famous ballerina Elizabeth Balletta, of the

Below: This superb gold cigarette case is decorated with laurel wreaths and swags of contrasting gold set with diamonds.

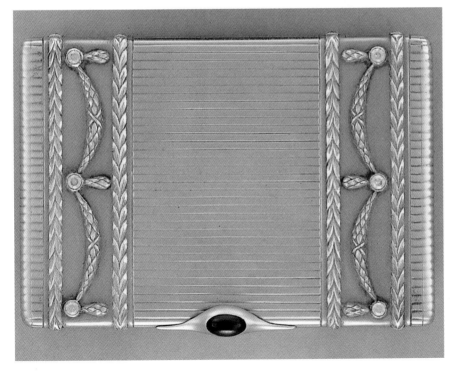

Above: One of the most famous and spectacular cigarette cases made by Fabergé, it also has a fascinating history. The case was given by Alice Keppel, *mistress of Edward VII, to the king in 1908, returned to her after his death, but later donated by Mrs Keppel to the Royal Collection. It is superbly enamelled in* *translucent dark blue over a wavy* guilloche *ground, with a snake in rose-cut diamonds on both sides.*

Imperial Michael Theatre, St Petersburg. She was greatly admired – on and off the stage – and this vanity case, which contains a gold pencil, lipstick tube and compartments for powder, was a gift from an ardent admirer, Grand Duke Alexei Alexandrovitch, brother of Tsar Alexander III. An inveterate womaniser, he was admiral-in-chief of the Russian Navy during the *débâcle* against the Japanese Navy in 1905; it was said of him that he preferred 'slow ships and fast women'.

FABERGÉ CIGARETTE CASES

Of all those made by Fabergé, the most famous and most characteristic boxes are the cigarette cases. They are often regarded as Fabergé's equivalent of the magnificent snuff-boxes made in eighteenth-century France, and it is certainly true that they share a common elegance and craftsmanship. What is particularly striking about Fabergé's cigarette cases is their restraint and simplicity, the stripping away of excess embellishment to reveal the essence of the object in a way that foreshadowed the style of the 1920s. As ever, Fabergé was ready to assimilate a variety of influences, but only as a starting-point for his own expression. Where he did copy, the source is obvious, as we have seen in numerous examples of his work. The cigarette cases are the

Below: Three elegant cigarette cases, two in nephrite and one in guilloche *enamel.*

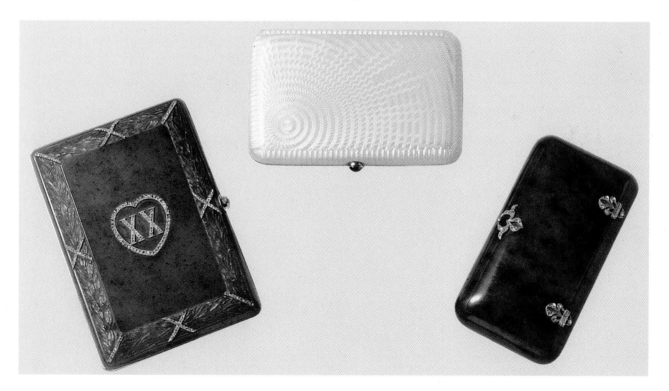

ultimate in the style Fabergé, the embodiment of chic, from the time when they were made to this day.

A superb example is the gold case with a blue, translucent enamel, which has a band of diamonds on both sides in the form of a serpent. This was a gift from the Edwardian beauty Alice Keppel to her lover, King Edward VII. Mrs Keppel, a regular visitor at Sandringham, was called to the dying king's deathbed and the love gift was returned to her by Queen Alexandra as a keepsake. She later gave it to Queen Mary so that it could be kept with the rest of the Fabergé collection at Sandringham.

FABERGÉ STONE FIGURES

Among the rarest items of Fabergé's output – and the most controversial – are the stone figures. Bainbridge estimated that only 50 were made, but later scholars, such as Alexander von Solodkoff, believe that the total may be closer to 80.

The figures are principally of Russian types, figures of non-Russian origin being the exception. The Russian types are realistic depictions of people drawn from daily life in St Petersburg: a burly carpenter, a jaunty street-sweeper, a massive coachman, a haughty cavalry officer. Some were not generic but of individuals: Nicholas II is said to have commissioned a figure of Pustinikov, the Cossack bodyguard of the Dowager Empress Marie, who accompanied the empress on all

Opposite: A marvellously lifelike figure of a vendor specialising in the sale of drinks.

Right: Another street-vendor figure, made from a variety of stones – a chalcedony apron, jasper boots, grey granite mittens and an obsidian and lapis-lazuli hat.

her journeys by car or sleigh. The Cossack had to 'sit' for his portrait, as it were, attending the Fabergé studios to be modelled in wax before the stone model could be made.

Many admirers of Fabergé's work draw a line at the figures, particularly the carvings of Russian types, which are often condemned as being mawkish and kitsch, inviting comparisons with garden gnomes or plaster ducks. They were popular at the time, however, often serving as table decorations in pre-revolutionary Russia, and were much admired by many English patrons. Lady Sackville had a mascot of a Russian driver of public vehicles *(izvoschik)* and took it everywhere.

FABERGÉ'S ANIMAL CARVINGS

The most brilliant use of Russia's store of semi-precious stones can be seen in Fabergé's carvings of animals, where the stones were carefully chosen to match the appearance or personality of the animal. Polished green nephrite was used for frogs, velvety-black obsidian for seals, pink aventurine quartz for horses, various shades of agate for dogs and cats. The artists who created the animal carvings did not strive to achieve a perfect replica of the animal, although the figures are usually convincingly realistic. The intention was to capture the essential character of the subject, which is achieved by portraying it in a characteristic pose, often with an endearing touch of humour.

The largest colllection of animal carvings belongs to Queen Elizabeth, and its origins are well known. The idea for the collection was born when Mrs Keppel, Edward VII's mistress, suggested to Bainbridge that a few carvings of some of the favourite animals kept at Sandringham might make an excellent birthday gift for Queen Alexandra.

Below right: A dormouse, in brown chalcedony, enjoying a nibble of gold straw. It has cabochon-sapphire eyes and platinum whiskers.

A CRITICAL ASSESSMENT

It must be admitted that Fabergé's work is not universally admired. Some dislike it because it seems to them to reek of a world of privilege; they find something irredeemably vulgar in what they see as the ostentatious display of wealth by the possession of luxurious, extravagant objects; they find something shocking in the concept of spending so much money, effort and time – years, for some of the Imperial eggs – on creating objects which they regard as mere jewelled baubles.

Those who take such a view will probably never be converted, but it should nevertheless

be remembered that Fabergé reflected the society in which he lived, just as the goldsmiths of the eighteenth century reflected their time. The objects made in eighteenth-century France and nineteenth-century Russia could only have been made then: they speak of the spirit of their age as convincingly as historical documents. Fabergé was also an innovator, particularly in the revolutionary concept of placing emphasis on craftsmanship and quality of design rather than on the intrinsic value of the materials used, and in achieving this with his *objets de fantasie* he also succeeded in creating a public demand for his work.

Below: The splendid shire horse Marshall was one of the animals modelled at Sandringham in 1907, and was part of the collection of Fabergé farmyard animals given by King Edward VII to his wife. It is of aventurine quartz, with cabochon-sapphire eyes.

Right: A figure of a Russian nobleman. Such figures are among the rarest items of Fabergé's output, and are also the most controversial.

A more serious charge is that Fabergé's work sometimes veered towards the kitsch. Critics point, for example, to a match-holder shaped as a pig, mounted on silver, and a silver table-lighter which is shaped like the head of a wolf which protrudes from a shawl, the flame issuing from the mouth. There is something overdone and faintly ridiculous about both pieces, which perfectly illustrate pure kitsch. Carrying the same degree of exaggeration is a toadstool, naturalistically carved in different colours of agate growing from a mound of unpolished material set with diamonds, the polished head of which can be lifted to reveal a gold-lined inkwell.

Perhaps the objects most likely to make the sensitive observer wince are the Russian national figures, which are made of coloured stones chosen to match the hair or clothes of the subject. These purely naturalistic studies suffer from a lifeless stiffness, while the more animated, almost cartoon-like, figures are sometimes embarrassingly whimsical. The same generous helping of whimsy can be seen in the animal carvings, where animals are cari-catured in a style that anticipates Walt Disney.

It may be that examples of this kind were in the mind of Ian Bennett when he was compiling Phaidon's *Encyclopaedia of Decorative Arts, 1890–1940*, in which he takes a highly critical view of Fabergé's work, dismissing it 'the rich man's plaster ducks'. He does, however, concede the 'unquestion-able technical brilliance and perfectly

Left: An egg-shaped bonbonnière, *some 7.6cm (3in) tall,, in a beautiful, mottled-brown agate, decorated with gold, flowered swags and scrolls. It is thought to have been inspired by a* bonbonnière *of the George II period.*

orchestrated use of materials' and the 'extra-ordinary workmanship' of Fabergé's work.

A tribute of the same kind was paid to Fabergé by Henry M Hawley, curator of the India Early Minshall Collection, Cleveland Museum of Art, when he wrote:

> *Even a limited study of the products of Fabergé's workshop indicates that technically they are unsurpassed in the history of European manufacture of objects in precious metals with enamel and jewelled decorations and hardstone carvings. Their only serious rivals are several Parisian and a handful of German workshops of the eighteenth century, and in at least one respect, the use of transparent enamels, Fabergé clearly exceeded all previous efforts. Thus it can be safely stated that the outstanding products of Carl Fabergé are technically the very best things of their kind ever to have been made in the West.*

A more personal accolade came from that ardent Fabergé devotee Queen Mary, wife of George V, a lady who kept her emotions well in check but was moved to say, while caressing one of Fabergé's cigarette cases, 'There is one thing about all Fabergé's pieces, they are so satisfying'.

Right: A lady's cigarette case in two-colour gold and enamel. The enamel is opalescent white over a wavy ground, decorated with laurel-leaf bands and arrow-linked wreaths.